CLASSIC TALES

Snow White
and the Seven Dwarfs

Retold by Sue Arengo

Illustrated by Susan Rowe

ELEMENTARY **3**

OXFORD UNIVERSITY PRESS

ONCE upon a time, on a cold winter's day, a queen sat by the window of her castle. She sat and made clothes for her baby. She wanted to have a little girl.

Sometimes she looked out of the window. Outside, the snow fell, and it was very cold.

Suddenly, she pricked her finger with her needle, and three drops of red blood fell from it.

'Red is a beautiful colour,' she thought.

Then she looked at the dark black wood of the trees outside and at the white snow.

'My little girl will be very beautiful,' thought the Queen. 'She will have skin as white as snow, hair as black as those trees and cheeks as red as blood.'

Soon the Queen had her baby, a little daughter. And the little girl had skin as white as snow, hair as black as trees in winter and cheeks as red as blood.

'Oh, dear little child,' said the Queen, 'you are very beautiful! I will call you Snow White.'

She loved the little girl very much. But when Snow White was only two years old, a very sad thing happened. The Queen was very ill and she died.

After a few years, Snow White's father, the King, married again. His new queen was beautiful, but she was also nasty and unkind. She thought that she was the most beautiful woman in the country.

'And I will *always* be the most beautiful woman in the country!' she said.

The new queen looked at Snow White. She saw that the little girl was very beautiful, and she was jealous. She saw the light in Snow White's eyes and she wanted to kill her.

The new queen had a magic mirror. Every day she stood in front of it and asked:

'Mirror, mirror, on the wall,
Who is the most beautiful of all?'
The mirror always answered:
'You are, Queen.'
But one day, when she asked this question, the mirror answered:
'Of all the women who stand tall,
You, Queen, are the most beautiful of all.
But listen now, for this is true:
Snow White is more beautiful than you.'

The Queen was very angry.

'When I see Snow White, I am ill!' she said. 'She must die. I never want to see her face again.'

She gave some money to a huntsman and said to him, 'Take Snow White into the forest and kill her. Do this or you will die. Go! Be quick! Bring me back her heart. Then I will know that she is dead.'

The huntsman did not want to do it, but he was afraid. So he took Snow White and together they walked far into the forest. He put his hand on his knife three times. But each time Snow White turned and looked at him, and he could not kill her.

At last, the huntsman said, 'Listen, Snow White. The Queen said that I must kill you. But I can't do it. Run, Snow White! Run far away into the forest. And do not come back to the castle.'

Then the huntsman killed a deer and took its heart.

'I will take this deer's heart back to the Queen,' he thought. 'And I will tell her that Snow White is dead.'

Snow White was alone and lost. She ran through the forest. She ran all day. Now it was late and she was afraid.

The forest was full of strange noises. She knew that there were wild animals there, but they did not come near her.

At last, Snow White came out of the forest. She saw a mountain, and at the foot of the mountain she saw a little house.

'I'll go and knock on the door,' she thought.
'Then perhaps a kind person will help me.'

'Hello!' she called. But there was no answer.
It was almost dark now, so she opened the door.

Inside, the furniture was very small, and there
was seven of everything: seven little chairs and
seven little beds. There were seven little cups on
the table, and seven plates of food.

'Perhaps seven little children live here,'
thought Snow White. 'But where are they?'

Snow White was very hungry, but she didn't want to take someone's dinner. So she ate a little from each plate, and she drank a little from each cup. Then she went upstairs and fell asleep on three of the little beds.

The house belonged to seven dwarfs. Every day the dwarfs went to the mountain and looked for gold. That night they finished their work and came home.

'Someone has eaten from our plates and drunk from our cups,' said one.

'Perhaps it was a mouse,' laughed the others. 'Come on! Let's take off our boots and sit down and eat.'

Then the youngest dwarf called from upstairs, 'Come quickly, everybody. Come and see. There is a young girl asleep on our beds. She is very beautiful.'

10

All the other dwarfs ran upstairs.

'Yes, she is very beautiful!' they said. 'Shhh! Don't wake her.' So that night they all slept downstairs by the fire.

In the morning, Snow White told them her story.

'Stay here with us,' said the dwarfs. 'The Queen is a very dangerous woman. You can never go back to your castle now.'

'Yes,' said the oldest dwarf. 'Stay. Please stay.'

'Thank you,' said Snow White. 'You are all very kind.'

So Snow White stayed and lived with the seven dwarfs. She cooked and cleaned and washed for them, and they were kind to her.

Every morning the dwarfs went to the mountain to look for gold.

'Be careful, Snow White,' they said when they left. 'The Queen is a very dangerous woman. She must not know that you are here. Don't leave the house and do not open the door to anyone.'

'The Queen will never find me,' said Snow White. 'She thinks that I am dead.'

The Queen did not speak to her magic mirror for a long time. But one day, she stood in front of it and asked:

> '*Mirror, mirror, on the wall,*
> *Who is the most beautiful of all?'*

And the mirror answered:

> '*You, Queen, are beautiful, it's true.*
> *But there is one more beautiful than you.*
> *Snow White's not dead. She's living still,*
> *In a house in the forest over the hill.*
> *And although you are beautiful, it's true,*
> *Snow White is more beautiful than you.'*

'What?' said the Queen. 'She's not dead? I'll kill the huntsman! And I'll kill Snow White too, when I find her.'

Then the Queen dressed as an old woman. She put some ribbons in a basket and left the castle secretly.

'Snow White will not know that it's me,' she laughed.

She walked quickly through the forest until she came to the little house at the foot of the mountain.

'Hello,' she called. 'Is anyone in?'

Snow White looked out of the window. 'What do you want?' she asked.

'Would you like to buy some ribbons, my dear?' said the old woman.

Snow White looked at the ribbons. They were beautiful ribbons, pink and blue and yellow.

'She's just a poor old woman,' thought Snow White. 'She can't hurt me.'

So she opened the door.

The old woman showed Snow White the ribbons.

'Look at these pink ones.'

'They're beautiful,' said Snow White.

'Here, I'll help you. I'll tie them for you.'

But the old woman tied the ribbons very tightly and Snow White could not breathe. She fell to the floor.

That night the dwarfs found her there. They saw the new ribbons and quickly untied them.

'What happened?' they asked.

Snow White told them about the old woman.

'That was not an old woman,' said the dwarfs. 'That was the Queen!'

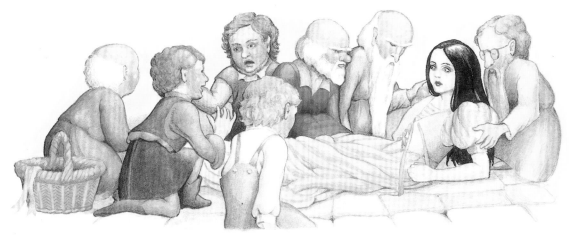

Back at the castle, the Queen stood in front of her magic mirror and asked:

> '*Mirror, mirror, on the wall,*
> *Who is the most beautiful of all?*'

But again the mirror answered:

> '*You, Queen, are beautiful, it's true.*
> *But there is one more beautiful than you.*
> *Snow White's not dead. She's living still,*
> *In a house in the forest over the hill.*
> *And although you are beautiful, it's true,*
> *Snow White is more beautiful than you.*'

'What?' said the Queen. 'Is she still not dead? Then I will go to her again.'

So the Queen dressed as another old woman. This time she put some poisoned combs in her basket.

At the dwarfs' house she called, 'Good morning! I've got some combs. Beautiful combs for your hair. Is anyone there?'

Snow White looked out of the window.

'I'm sorry, old woman,' she said, 'but you can't come into the house.'

'Well, you can come to the door and look, can't you?' said the old woman.

Snow White thought for a minute. She wanted to see the combs very much.

'All right,' she said, and she went downstairs and opened the door.

The old woman opened her basket and showed Snow White the poisoned combs.

'I like that pink comb,' said Snow White.

'Do you?' said the old woman. 'Here, my dear. I'll put it in your hair.'

Then she stuck the poisoned comb into Snow White's head and poor Snow White fell to the floor.

That night the dwarfs found
her. They saw the comb and
pulled it from her hair.

'What happened?' they asked.

Snow White told them about
the old woman.

'That was the Queen again!'
said the oldest dwarf. 'Snow White, you must
remember: do not open the door to anyone.'

Back at the castle, the Queen stood before the
magic mirror and asked:

> 'Mirror, mirror, on the wall,
> Who is the most beautiful of all?'

But again the mirror answered:

> 'You, Queen, are beautiful, it's true.
> But there is one more beautiful than you.
> Snow White's not dead. She's living still,
> In a house in the forest over the hill.
> And although you are beautiful, it's true,
> Snow White is more beautiful than you.'

'Is she still alive?' said the Queen. 'Then I'll go
to her again. I'll give her a poisoned apple.'

The Queen dressed as a farmer's wife and went to the dwarfs' cottage. But Snow White did not want to open the door.

'I'm sorry, old woman,' she called. 'You can't come in. The dwarfs said that I must not open the door.'

Then the old woman showed her the poisoned apple.

'I'm sorry, old woman,' said Snow White. 'I haven't got any money.'

'You don't have to buy it, dear,' said the old woman. 'I'll give it to you for nothing.'

'Hm,' thought Snow White, 'the apple looks very nice.'

'Don't be afraid,' said the old woman. It's not poisoned. Look, I'll cut it in two. I'll eat this green half and you can have the beautiful red half. See? There's no danger.'

'All right,' said Snow White. 'Thank you, old woman.' And she took the red half and began to eat.

But when the first piece of the poisoned apple was in her mouth, she fell to the floor.

'Ha!' laughed the old woman. 'Goodbye for ever, Snow White.'

Back at the castle, the Queen asked her mirror:
'Mirror, mirror, on the wall,
Who is the most beautiful of all?'
And now at last the mirror answered:
'You are, Queen.'
That night, the dwarfs returned and found
Snow White on the floor. They tried to wake her,
but she did not move or open her eyes.

'This time she is dead,' said the oldest dwarf.
'She has gone from us for ever.'

For three days and nights the dwarfs sat by
Snow White. They knew that she was dead, but
they did not want to bury her.

'She looks as if she is only asleep,' they said.
'We can't bury her in the ground.'

So they made a glass box, put Snow White in it
and carried her up the mountain.

'She can lie here,' said the oldest dwarf. 'Then
we can come and see her every day.'

On the side of the box the dwarfs wrote in gold:

HERE LIES SNOW WHITE, THE DAUGHTER OF A KING

– and one dwarf always sat with her, day and night.

Time went by, but Snow White's skin was still as white as snow. Her cheeks were still as red as blood and her hair was still as black as trees in winter.

Then one day, a prince came by with some friends. When he saw Snow White, he fell in love with her at once.

'I want to take her with me,' he said to the dwarf. 'I will give you anything!'

'No,' said the dwarf. 'Snow White belongs to us.'

But the Prince asked again and again.

'Can I take her with me? Please.'

At last, the dwarf said, 'Wait here. I will go and get my brothers.'

Then all the dwarfs came and stood in front of the Prince.

'I am in love with her,' said the Prince. 'I can't live without her.'

'Yes,' said the oldest dwarf. 'You love Snow White. I can see it in your face. And we must give her to you. You are a prince and she is a princess, the daughter of a king. We are only poor dwarfs.'

'Take all my gold,' said the Prince.

'No,' said the old dwarf. 'We don't want anything. We will give her to you because you love her.'

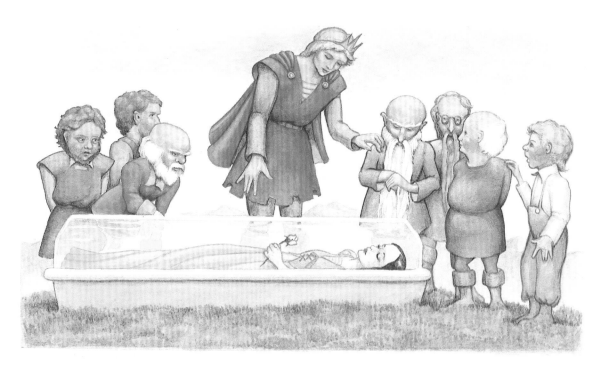

The dwarfs began to carry the glass box down the mountain. But they tripped near a tree and the box fell.

At that moment, the piece of apple fell out of Snow White's mouth.

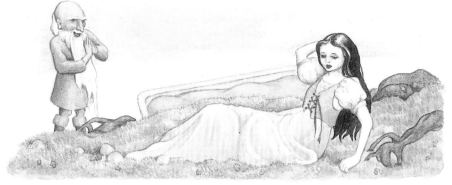

She opened her eyes and saw the Prince. When she saw him, she fell in love with him at once.

'Here you see your husband,' said the Prince. 'Will you be my wife?'

'Yes,' she said.

So Snow White said goodbye to her friends the dwarfs, and went away with the Prince.

In December they were married and there was a big party. Lots of important people came, and one of these important people was the jealous Queen.

When she saw Snow White, she couldn't believe her eyes.

'What is this?' she said. 'Is Snow White still alive?'

She was very angry. When she saw Snow White and the Prince, she was jealous. She ran out of the castle and no one saw her again.

Snow White loved the Prince, and he loved her. In time, they had seven children, and they all lived happily ever after.

Exercises

1 Who is it? Read and guess.

1 She was very beautiful and was the daughter of a king.
2 They said, 'Do not open the door to anyone.'
3 He killed a deer.
4 She was very beautiful, but nasty and unkind. She was the wife of a king.
5 He fell in love with Snow White at once.

2 Put the words in the correct list.

| an apple | ~~black~~ | castle | combs | forest |
| house | mountain | red | ribbons | white |

Colours	The Queen gives Snow White...	Places in the story
black	....	....
....	....	....
....	....	....
		....

3 Choose the right answer.

1 Snow White was called Snow White because …

2 The Queen wanted to kill Snow White because …

3 The seven dwarfs wanted Snow White to live with them because …

4 The dwarfs gave Snow White to the Prince because …

5 The Queen ran out of the castle because …

Snow White was more beautiful than her.

he loved her.

she was jealous of Snow White and the Prince.

her skin was as white as snow.

they knew that the Queen wanted to kill her.

4 Do the '7' puzzle and find the missing word.

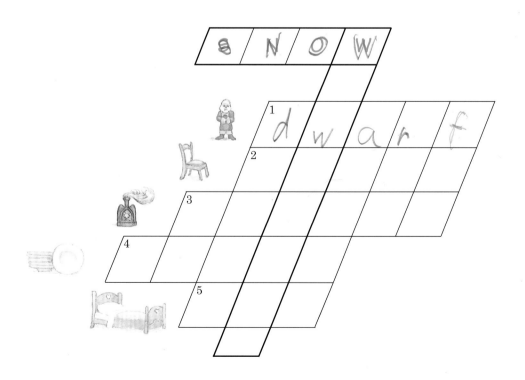

29

Glossary

boots

breathe   to take in air and push it out again, through your mouth or nose

bury   to put something under the ground

cheeks   the sides of your face

combs

dwarf   a very small man or woman

farmer
A **farmer** and his wife –

forest

furniture

heart

huntsman

jealous   when you are **jealous**, you want to have something which belongs to another person

knife

lost   when you are **lost**, you don't know where you are

mirror   a piece of glass which you can look in and see yourself

mouse

needle

poison

prick
She has **pricked** her finger –

ribbons

secretly   if you do something
secretly, nobody sees you do
it

skin   our bodies are covered
in **skin**

stuck   past tense of **stick:**
to push

tie
He's **tying**   He has **untied**
his shoe –   his shoe –

tightly
The ribbons are tied very
tightly –

trip   to fall

untie   see **tie**

wild animals   animals which
do not live with people

wood   trees are made of **wood**

OXFORD
UNIVERSITY PRESS

Great Clarendon Street, Oxford OX2 6DP

Oxford University Press is a department of the University of Oxford.
It furthers the University's objective of excellence in research, scholarship,
and education by publishing worldwide in

Oxford New York

Auckland Cape Town Dar es Salaam Hong Kong Karachi
Kuala Lumpur Madrid Melbourne Mexico City Nairobi
New Delhi Shanghai Taipei Toronto

With offices in

Argentina Austria Brazil Chile Czech Republic France Greece
Guatemala Hungary Italy Japan Poland Portugal Singapore
South Korea Switzerland Thailand Turkey Ukraine Vietnam

OXFORD and OXFORD ENGLISH are registered trade marks of
Oxford University Press in the UK and in certain other countries

© Oxford University Press 1995

ISBN: 978 0 19 422010 1

A recorded reading of this *Classic Tale* is available on cassette in either
British or American English. Each cassette features two stories.
Beauty and the Beast and *Snow White and the Seven Dwarfs*
978 0 19 422017 0 (British English) 978 0 19 422035 4 (American English)

An Activity Book is also available for this title ISBN: 978 0 19 422066 8

Printed in Hong Kong

ACKNOWLEDGEMENTS
Original story retold by: Sue Arengo
Illustrated by: Susan Rowe